SPEEDY & CHEDDY
take on
Old Town Marblehead

Speedy and Cheddy take on Old Town Marblehead
Authored by Lucia Fontinel & Isaiah Moskowitz

© 2024 Lucia Fontinel and Isaiah Moskowitz

ISBN 979-8-218-44525-6

All rights reserved.

"

Dedicated to our parents Elizabeth & Saul Moskowitz, Robert & Helen Fontinel and to all of the sweet Cardinal Visits.

This is also dedicated to Auntie Susan, Auntie Stephanie and Danielle from Blue's Bridge. 10% of the proceeds from this book will go to Blue's Bridge to help other kitties, squirrels and birdies with their rescue journey.

Last but not least thank you to Rose Ann Fontinel for her inspiration, creativity and guidance and Hameo for bringing Speedy and Cheddy to life with her amazing illustrations.

We found Cheddy & Speedy in Malden, MA on a rainy day in May with their sisters Spanky and Gemma Jet Jumper. KITTIES! They scattered from under the fence to the grille. We quickly went into action to rescue them and look for their mom.

Then we found homes for the Kitties. Gemma Jet Jumper was off to Auntie Stephanie's house in Cambridge to be a City Kitty, Spanky moved to a castle of greatness and Speedy & Cheddy were ready to take on Marblehead with us.

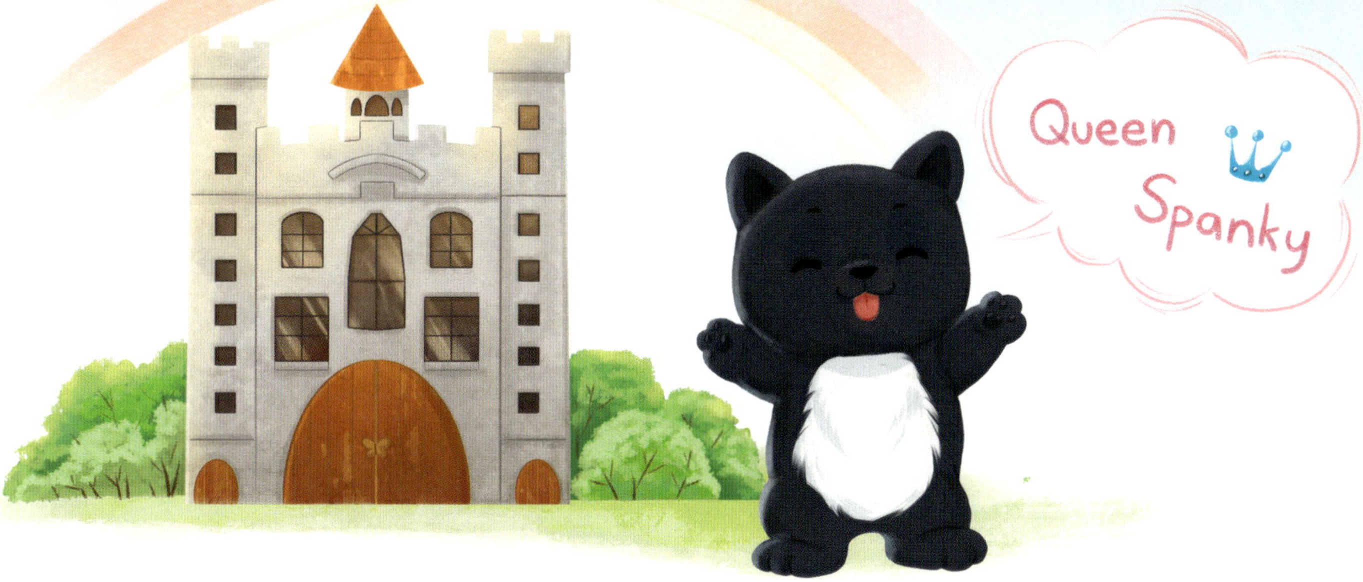

Your New Home Will Be Great!

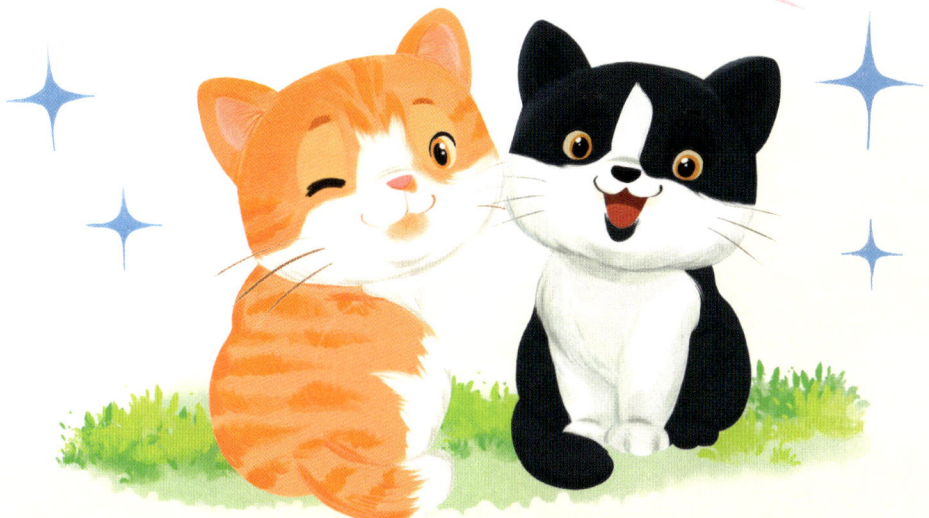

SPEEDY AND CHEDDY ARE OFF
TO EXPLORE OLD TOWN
MARBLEHEAD!

"Hey, can I get a Meowtini? Shaken not purred, of course. Make it a Maddie's pour"

Along the way Speedy and Cheddy meet some of their friends and invite them over for treats.

Speedy and Cheddy watch 4th of July fireworks from Fort Sewall with their pals Kitty and King! Check out those fireworks — they are so Cat-tab-u-lous! Turn up the mewsic and let's get this pawty started!

Speedy and Cheddy run into Gus and Rocky at the Old Town House. Cheddy Says "Wait a Meow-ment, don't forget to Vote".

Gus says back "I'm on it, voting Santa Claws for President!"

Rocky says "Me too, you've got to be Kitten me. How Claw-some is that?"

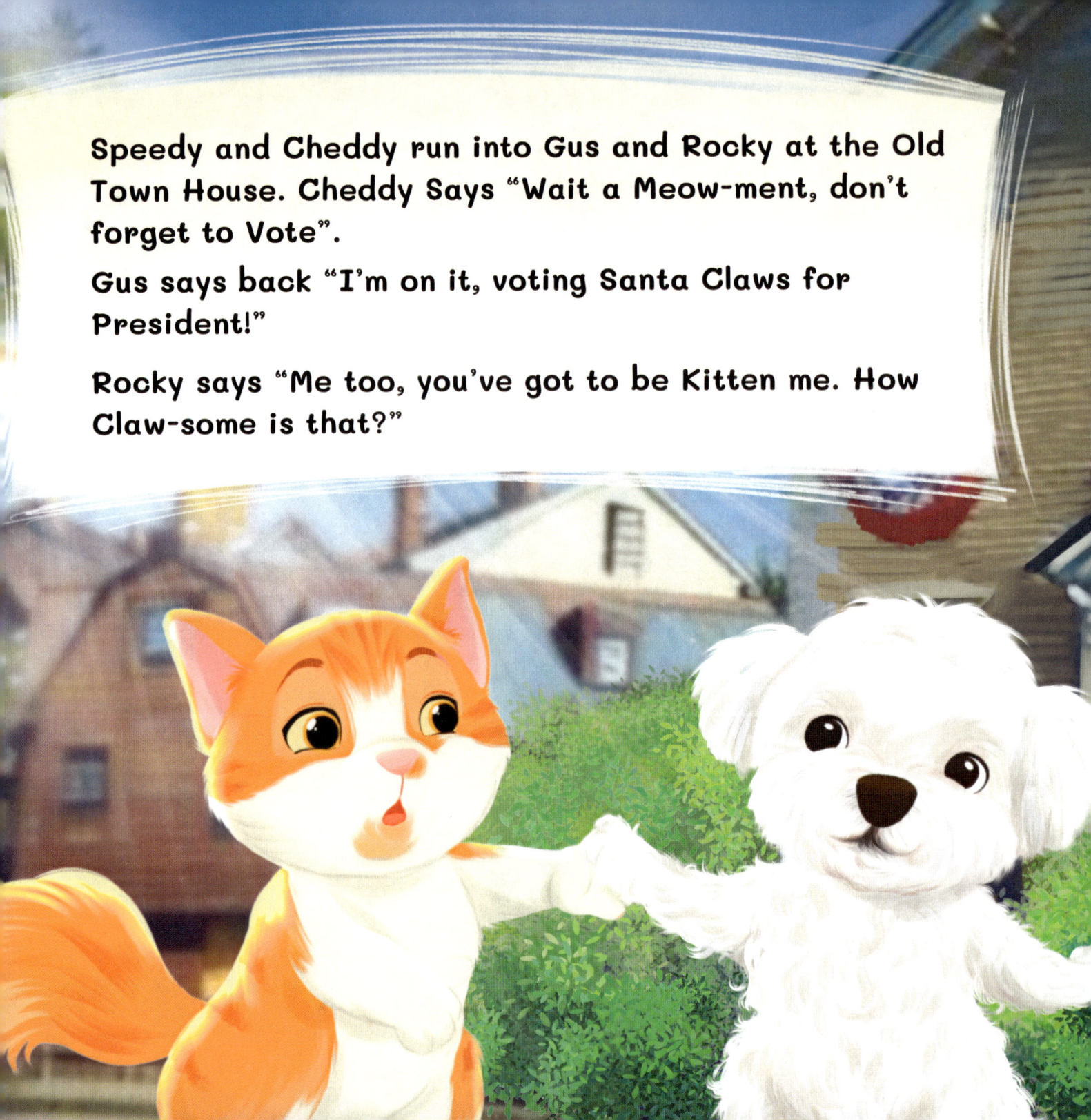

We love Speedy and Cheddy and they love Old Town Marblehead. Thank you for taking on Marblehead with Speedy and Cheddy and I wonder where Speedy and Cheddy will go next???